LIBYA: FIVE YEARS AFTER GHADAFI

JOINT HEARING

BEFORE THE

SUBCOMMITTEE ON
THE MIDDLE EAST AND NORTH AFRICA

AND THE

SUBCOMMITTEE ON TERRORISM,
NONPROLIFERATION, AND TRADE

OF THE

COMMITTEE ON FOREIGN AFFAIRS
HOUSE OF REPRESENTATIVES

ONE HUNDRED FOURTEENTH CONGRESS

SECOND SESSION

———

NOVEMBER 30, 2016

———

Serial No. 114–238

———

Printed for the use of the Committee on Foreign Affairs

Available via the World Wide Web: http://www.foreignaffairs.house.gov/ or
http://www.gpo.gov/fdsys/

———

U.S. GOVERNMENT PUBLISHING OFFICE

22–863PDF   WASHINGTON : 2017

For sale by the Superintendent of Documents, U.S. Government Publishing Office
Internet: bookstore.gpo.gov   Phone: toll free (866) 512–1800; DC area (202) 512–1800
Fax: (202) 512–2104   Mail: Stop IDCC, Washington, DC 20402–0001

(III)

CONTENTS

LIBYA: FIVE YEARS AFTER GHADAFI

WEDNESDAY, NOVEMBER 30, 2016

HOUSE OF REPRESENTATIVES,
SUBCOMMITTEE ON THE MIDDLE EAST AND NORTH AFRICA AND
SUBCOMMITTEE ON TERRORISM, NONPROLIFERATION, AND TRADE,
COMMITTEE ON FOREIGN AFFAIRS,
Washington, DC.

The subcommittees met, pursuant to notice, at 11:26 a.m., in room 2172, Rayburn House Office Building, Hon. Ileana Ros-Lehtinen (chairman of the Subcommittee on the Middle East and North Africa) presiding.

Ms. ROS-LEHTINEN. The subcommittees will come to order. We will start with our opening statements. Our good friends on the other side are still caucusing. We have tried to wait as long as possible, but when Mr. Meadows said that he was leaving, that was it. We said we have got to start, time is of the essence. So we will do a little bit of business and hear from our witness. Thank you. And then we will wait for our colleagues to come back.

So after recognizing myself, and when they come in, Ranking Member Deutch and Ranking Member Keating for 5 minutes each for our opening statements, I will recognize other members seeking recognition for 1 minute. We will start with that process now. We will then hear from our witness and, without objection, the witness' prepared statement will be made a part of the record. Members may have 5 days to insert statements and questions for the record subject to the length limitation in the rules.

Before beginning my opening statement, I would first like to take a moment to acknowledge the other chairman of this joint subcommittee hearing, Judge Poe, who could not be with us this morning as he continues to undergo treatment for leukemia. I know that all of our thoughts and prayers are with Judge Poe as he fights this disease, we wish him the best. I have his opening statement, without objection, it will be made a part of the record now.

The Chair recognizes herself for 5 minutes.

December 17 marks the 1-year anniversary of the Libyan Political Agreement, making this an opportune time to review the administration's policy in Libya. While this administration first participated in the intervention in Libya in 2011, many of us expressed concern with the administration's lack of clearly articulated objectives, a post-intervention plan, and even an explanation about how it fit U.S. national security interests. Many of our worst fears have come to fruition, as more than 5 years after Ghadafi's death, Libya is embroiled in a difficult civil war that shows no sign

(1)

of abatement. If anything, it has only gotten worse since the U.N.-brokered agreement. Libya is more politically divided than ever, its economy is in a free fall, and terrorist groups and criminals continue to exploit the power vacuum.

Multiple governing entities and their allied militias and armed forces compete for power while the U.N.-backed unity government, known as the Government of National Accord, remains unable to provide basic security and basic services to the people of Libya. Criminals and terrorist groups, including ISIS, al-Qaeda and so many others, take advantage of the chaos, securing their own territory and using Libya as a launching pad for smuggling, human trafficking, and terror attacks—endangering Libya's neighbors, such as Egypt and Tunisia. Libya is now the main transit point for migrants trying to reach Europe, and with little border security or governance, many are rightly concerned by the potential of terrorists reaching our own shores. While reports say that forces are close to retaking Sirte from ISIS, we should not allow this news to disguise the sad reality: ISIS' presence in Libya is far from being eliminated. ISIS, al-Qaeda, Ansar al-Sharia, the group responsible for the 2012 Benghazi attack, as well as others, all continue to maintain cells throughout the country.

In a positive development, I was relieved to see the announcement last month that the Organization for the Prohibition of Chemical Weapons was able to remove Libya's remaining chemical weapons equipment. Another welcome development, if accurate, is the reported killing by French air strikes of the Algerian jihadist known as the ''one-eyed terrorist.'' He is said to have been responsible for organizing terrorist attacks in Libya, Algeria and Mali, so many other places, and had funneled millions of dollars to al-Qaeda. France's air strikes highlight the stakes that many outside actors have in Libya. Russia, Egypt, Saudi Arabia, the UAE, and others, continue to support Khalifa Haftar, the former Libyan National Army general who recently claimed victory in Benghazi and who was just in Moscow discussing Russian military assistance. Reports indicate that at least four countries have Special Forces on the ground in Libya right now, including our own, and, in some cases, are assisting forces on both sides of Libya's civil war. It is also worth noting that in recent months Haftar has seized many of the ports in Libya's oil crescent, which is Libya's main source of revenue.

With additional violence on the horizon, potentially between eastern and western forces, Haftar's role must be addressed in Libya's political dialogue—a dialogue that should come sooner rather than later. Since the unity government took up residence in Tripoli in March, it has struggled to provide the kind of basic services and security that could engender the support that it needs in order to consolidate power. And as long as it keeps struggling in the west while its rival governing entities and security forces keep operating and making gains in the east, any chance that the current peace process had at succeeding will continue to be undermined.

As we approach the 1-year anniversary of the Libyan Political Agreement, it is clear that the status quo in Libya is unsustainable, and that there must be a new and revitalized attempt at reconciling all Libyan stakeholders.

I look forward to hearing from our witness on exactly how the administration is working to help get that peace process back on track, the status of our counterterrorism operation against ISIS and others, and what kind of changes to our Libya policy and assistance we should expect moving forward.

And I am now pleased to yield to members for their opening statements. I will turn to Mr. Chabot of Ohio.

Mr. CHABOT. Thank you, Madam Chair. Thank you for holding this important hearing. Despite Libya's obviously geopolitical importance, it has really not received the public attention that it deserves. President Obama has called his administration's failure to adequately plan for a post-Ghadafi Libya the worst mistake of his presidency. The word ''mistake'' really doesn't begin to capture the situation in Libya, which is a catastrophic failure.

Back in August 2012, I spent the better part of a day and a half with Ambassador Stevens in Tripoli. This was about a month before he was brutally murdered along with three other brave Americans. Of course the administration misled the American people at that time by saying that this was caused by some video. And we also later learned that Ambassador Stevens and his people had sought help and better security and more protection, and that they were basically ignored by their higher-ups in the State Department.

Libya's now engulfed in not one but two civil wars, the chaos has spread to Mali, and now both countries have become safe havens for al-Qaeda and ISIS. When the so-called Arab Spring spread to Libya in 2011, we were told a military intervention to overthrow Muammar Ghadafi was essential to our national security. We were told by the Obama administration that we could, in effect, lead from behind, and the costs of intervention would largely be borne by our allies. And finally, we were told Libya could easily be rebuilt and stabilized basically on the cheap. As it turns out, none of these things were true and I eagerly await the administration's views on these things and many others that we will question them.

And thank you, again, for holding this hearing.

Ms. ROS-LEHTINEN. Thank you very much, Mr. Chabot.

Do any members wish to make an opening statement?

If not, let me introduce our witness. I am pleased to welcome Mr. Jonathan Winer who serves as the State Department's special envoy for Libya, as well as senior adviser for MEK resettlement. Thank you for your work on that. He was previously the U.S. Deputy Assistant Secretary of State for international law enforcement. We welcome you to our subcommittee.

And for the record, Chairman Poe and I invited DOD officials to testify at our hearing, but the Department of Defense failed to respond to our invitation. Did not offer a witness. So we thank you for being here, sir. And we will turn to you for your opening statement, Mr. Winer.

STATEMENT OF MR. JONATHAN WINER, SPECIAL ENVOY FOR LIBYA, BUREAU OF NEAR EASTERN AFFAIRS, U.S. DEPARTMENT OF STATE

Mr. WINER. You are welcome, Madam Chairman.

Chairman Ros-Lehtinen——

Ms. Ros-Lehtinen. If you could put that microphone a little bit closer.

Mr. Winer. Sure. Chairman Ros-Lehtinen, Chairman Poe, Ranking Member Deutch, Ranking Member Keating, and distinguished members of the committees, I am honored by the opportunity to appear before you today to discuss U.S. foreign policy on Libya. Thank you.

During my service as special envoy for Libya, our policy has centered on promoting the ability of Libyans to maintain a stable, unified, and inclusive government that can both defeat ISIL and other terrorist groups, and simultaneously meet the security, economic, and humanitarian needs of the Libyan people.

After 42 years of Muammar Ghadafi's erratic rule, and 5 years since the country cast off his shackles, Libya has made some, but not enough progress in reaching these goals. Libya's post-Ghadafi institutions have not provided sufficient stability and opportunity for the Libyan people; but they have made some visible progress against terrorism and they still have an opportunity to move forward in securing a more functional national transitional government. Libya needs to move forward on both goals, neither objective is sustainable without the other.

Since the signing of the Libyan Political Agreement in Skhirat, Morocco on December 17, 2015, the Government of National Accord, or GNA, led by Prime Minister Fayez al-Sarraj has been a steadfast partner of the United States and the international community against ISIL.

A year ago, before the Skhirat Agreement, ISIL was expanding its presence in Libya, capturing 90 miles of prime Mediterranean coastline around the coastal city of Sirte, a stone's throw away from Europe's southern shores. A year later the picture looks very different. Now, due to the bravery of GNA-aligned Libyan soldiers supported since this summer by the skill of U.S. forces, who have conducted more than 450 air strikes coordinated with our Libyan partners, ISIL controls just a few city blocks in Sirte. And its grasp on even this sliver of Libyan territory is tenuous. In Benghazi and in Libya's east, ISIL and other terrorist groups in other parts of Libya have also been pushed back. In Benghazi and Libya's east, this has been due to sustained efforts by equally brave Libyan soldiers.

So we have seen Libyan soldiers in different parts of the country and with different political orientations taking on terrorism in different parts of Libya and what was a substantial presence of ISIL in terms of its control of territory in Libya is now all but eliminated. The gains against ISIL are real. They could also be reversible if Libyans do not come together to participate in the GNA and to help it perform its work for the Libyan people, and to unify against the common threat to all. This is true today for the transitional GNA, it will be true for the next Libyan Government that is formed after the country moves ahead with elections sometime next year, or in early 2018.

If Libyans choose to fight each other instead of uniting, they risk increasing the probability that ISIL and other violent extremists in its mold will be back. Accordingly, we are continuing our work seeking to broaden support for a common political path forward to build a more capable government and to unify and professionalize Libya's armed forces. We see no military solution to Libya's political divisions; sustainable security solutions require sustainable political solutions.

We also need to keep working with Libyans on getting oil flowing and stabilizing its economy. If Libya can get back to producing even 1 million barrels a day out of its previous 1.6 million barrel-per-day capacity, it could easily provide the Libyan people the funds they need for food, health care, education, and other basic needs. Sustainable economic success, too, requires sustainable political solutions. Continuing intensive mediation to ensure the political process moves forward will be critical. Libyans will continue to look to the U.S. for our help as the GNA moves forward in addressing these challenges, and we must be prepared to give it.

Ms. Chairman, Mr. Chairman, and members of the committee, the U.S. Government remains deeply engaged in Libya. We have shared national security interests in defeating ISIL. The U.S. supports the aspirations of the Libyan people for a united, inclusive, and responsive national government capable of overcoming the country's significant challenges and political divisions.

Thank you for the opportunity to testify. I look forward to answering any questions you may have.

[The prepared statement of Mr. Winer follows:]

Statement for the Record
Jonathan M. Winer, U.S. Special Envoy for Libya
House Foreign Affairs Committee
Sub-Committees on the Middle East & North Africa and
Terrorism, Nonproliferation & Trade
November 30, 2016

Chairman Ros-Lehtinen, Chairman Poe, Ranking Member Deutch, Ranking Member Keating, and distinguished members of the committees, thank you for the opportunity to appear before you today to discuss U.S. foreign policy on Libya.

During my service as Special Envoy for Libya, our policy has centered on promoting the ability of Libyans to maintain a stable, unified, and inclusive government that can both defeat ISIL and other terrorist groups and simultaneously meet the security, economic, and humanitarian needs of the Libyan people.

After 42 years of Mummar Qaddafi's erratic rule and five years since the country cast off his shackles, Libya has made some but not enough progress in reaching these goals. Libya's post-Qaddafi institutions have not provided sufficient stability and opportunity for the Libyan people. But Libyans have made some visible progress against terrorism. And they still have an opportunity to move forward in securing a more functional national transitional government. Libya needs to move forward on both goals: neither objective is sustainable without the other.

Since the signing of the Libyan Political Agreement in Skhirat, Morocco on December 17, 2015, the Government of National Accord (GNA) led by Prime Minister Fayez al-Sarraj has been a steadfast partner of the United States and the international community against ISIL. A year ago, before the Skhirat Agreement, ISIL was expanding, capturing 90 miles of Mediterranean coastline around the coast city of Sirte – a stone's-throw away from Europe's southern shores.

A year later, the picture looks very different. Now, due to the bravery of GNA-aligned Libyan fighters, supported since this summer by the skill of U.S. forces who have conducted more than 450 airstrikes, coordinated with our Libyan partners, ISIL controls just a few city blocks in Sirte. And its grasp on even this sliver of territory is tenuous. ISIL and other terrorist groups in other parts of Libya have also been pushed back. In Benghazi and in Libya's East, this has been due to sustained efforts by equally brave Libyan fighters. The counter-terrorism terrain remains complex, and the fight is far from over. The gains against ISIL are real.

But they also could be reversible, if Libyans do not come together to participate in the Government of National Accord and to help it perform its work for the Libyan people and to unify against the common threat to all. This is true today for the transitional Government of National Accord. It will be true for the next Libyan government that is formed after the country moves ahead with elections sometime next year or in early 2018.

ISIL has been dramatically weakened through its extensive losses in Sirte and Benghazi, and further losses in Sabratha, Derna, and elsewhere in Libya. Many hundreds of terrorists have died in these battles. But most of those who have not been killed probably have stayed in Libya and gone underground, forming cells elsewhere in the country. We believe they are waiting for opportunities to engage in further attacks in Libya or its neighbors, and if possible to reassert ISIL geographically. Political divisions among Libyans let ISIL in the first time. And unfortunately, Libyans still remain divided. The United States and other countries with a stake in seeing Libya succeed can help them bridge differences and focus on the real enemy, ISIL and other terrorist groups. To keep ISIL and other terrorist groups in Libya on their heels, we must work with the Libyan people and other like-minded countries to help Prime Minister al-Sarraj broaden support for a common political path forward, build a capable government, and unify and professionalize Libya's security forces. The security of Libya and the region and our own national security interests depend on it.

Libya's challenges would be profound for any government, and they are especially difficult for the GNA, which seeks to build consensus and which has to build capacity starting nearly from scratch. The GNA's Presidency Council moved to Tripoli on March 30 where it was welcomed by many Libyans who want an end to the chaos and fighting. Since its arrival the GNA has begun the critical work of rebuilding the Libyan state, but it still faces some opposition in the country and obstacles to its ability to govern. The potential for renewed fighting among Libyans remains a very real concern. To turn their attention to the fight against their common enemy, ISIL, we believe it essential that Libyans choose to make the national reconciliation they envisioned in the Political Agreement a reality.

Durable and broad political reconciliation remain essential for the Government of National Accord – or any other future Libyan government – to function. While the House of Representatives (HoR) voted on January 25 to approve the entire Political Agreement, with the exception of one article regarding who would be the head of the military, and Prime Minister al-Sarraj's nine-member GNA Presidency Council, it has never endorsed a GNA Cabinet or acted to amend the country's Constitutional Declaration. Libyans need to agree on a Cabinet so that Libyans in all parts of the country – east, west and south – can join in rebuilding their nation. It is critical that the international community remain aligned and speak with one voice in support of the GNA and the Libyan Political Agreement, and continue to support one Libyan-led and UN-facilitated political process.

The United States has offered its strong support to the Political Agreement and the GNA. A unity government that brings disparate parties and armed factions under one roof is the best way forward for Libya. International support for the GNA has consistently been strong; the United States, United Nations, EU, Arab League, and virtually all of the key European and Middle Eastern countries have expressed their support for the GNA, as echoed through adoption of UN Security Council resolution (UNSCR) 2259 which endorsed the GNA as the sole legitimate government of Libya.

We see no military solution to Libya's political divisions, no sustainable means to dominate by force. Sustainable progress will only be possible through Libyans addressing political differences. In the near term, intensive mediation to ensure the political process moves forward will be critical. We will continue to encourage Libyan parties to form a unified civilian command under the Political Agreement for unified military forces which operate under a form of joint command which reflects the country's diversity and regions and promotes security for all civilians.

Libya will need to build integrated military forces on a national basis, incorporating professional military personnel who functioned as professionals during the Qaddafi period, and including a range of qualified Libyan soldiers. In Tripoli, the GNA must develop a reliable, professional force to replace the patchwork of militias that continue to provide security on a neighborhood-by-neighborhood basis in Tripoli. We and other countries will support Prime Minister al-Sarraj as he builds the Presidential Guard under the leadership of Brigadier General Nakua to improve security in Tripoli. I have met Nakua and found him impressive and ready to take on the challenge. The next step is to select professional, vetted personnel and advance to training and equipping this force. The international community should partner with and provide assistance to this important institution.

The Libyans also need international support as they work to reform their economy and to strengthen their economic institutions. Without such steps, Libya's current economic course is unsustainable, and risks leading to further economic and humanitarian crisis that threatens to make Libya's existing security problems far worse.

To counter these risks, the GNA and the Central Bank of Libya, the Audit Bureau, and the National Oil Corporation must join together to stabilize and rebuild Libya's economy. For this reason, the United States helped bring Libyans together for focused economic meetings in London and Rome in October and November. The Libyans understand they need to finalize and operationalize a budget and address the growing disparity between the official and black market currency exchange rates. There are both monetary and fiscal reforms that would make a difference. But the most important step they could take to do this would be get oil production and exports back up to levels that can fund a reasonable budget and halt the rapid depletion of Libya's foreign reserves. This is achievable, if those with control over these resources choose the right path to turn Libya's oil-fields and pipelines back on.

In keeping with UN Security Council resolutions, the United States and other countries will continue to take vigorous action to prevent attempts to conduct transactions in Libyan oil outside legitimate channels. Such transactions are illegal under Libyan as well as international law. They invite massive corruption. They also would cause great harm to Libya's economy, risk fracturing the country, and could spark civil conflict over resources. Libyans could instead choose to cooperate with one another to produce oil, and work together to build a government which ensures that Libya's wealth is spent to benefit all of its people, transparently, and with effective controls to counter corruption and abuse. The United States and many other countries, as well as the IMF and World Bank among others are ready and willing to help – but the Libyan people need their leaders to take the first steps on the economic issues in order for help from others to make a difference.

Looking ahead, we also should support Libyans to build consensus on a calendar for a Constitutional referendum and legislative and executive elections in 2017. The Political Agreement is a transitional roadmap, and we are at the half-way point of the GNA's intended span. The Political Agreement's proponents and detractors alike agree on the need to move ahead to a new, elected government.

We must help them work together toward realizing a stable, peaceful transition that includes national elections.

In 2017, we will also need to support the Libyans as they stabilize post-ISIL Sirte. The Administration recently amended its FY 2017 budget request to Congress to provide the resources necessary to support U.S. engagement in the effort to counter ISIL in the region, including in Libya. For Libya, the Administration is seeking $148.0 million in FY 2017 foreign assistance to provide the United States government with the flexibility necessary to respond quickly to Libya's stabilization requirements in places like Sirte given the rapid progress GNA aligned forces have made to eradicate ISIL from the city and surrounding areas. Our foreign assistance in Libya advances stabilization in key communities, expands the security envelope east and south, and supports efforts to counter ISIL in key strongholds and vulnerable areas while also targeting the group's ability to recruit foreign fighters, obtain financing, and spread its message globally. These resources are critical to advancing our national security interests in Libya.

We must remain steadfast in our support for our Libyan counter-ISIL partners after Sirte is liberated. We cannot allow a vacuum in which violent extremists re-emerge. Stabilizing Sirte post-ISIL will require a collective and coordinated effort. We and partner nations, in coordination with UN Support Mission in Libya (UNSMIL) are working with the GNA to support a Libyan plan to stabilize Sirte after ISIL's defeat, including how we can help the Libyans with removal of UXO and IEDs. We will need to work together to address the return of IDPs to Sirte – virtually the entire population of approximately 100,000, in a safe way.

Chairman Ros-Lehtinen, Chairman Poe, and members of the Committees: as I described at the outset today, the U.S. government is deeply engaged with Libya because we have shared national security interests, including defeating ISIL. The United States also supports the aspirations of the Libyan people for a united, inclusive, and responsive national government capable of overcoming the country's significant challenges and political divisions. Thank you for the opportunity to testify. I look forward to answering any questions you have.

Mr. CHABOT [presiding]. Thank you, Mr. Winer.

Ms. Ros-Lehtinen had to go out. I am filling in for her at this time. So I will recognize myself for 5 minutes.

Her first question would have been, and I will ask it at this time, please describe the various violent Islamist extremist and terrorist groups currently operating in Libya. Who are they? How many fighters does each group have? What are their goals? And anything else that you think would be relevant and helpful for this committee to understand.

Mr. WINER. Sure. There are four major groups that are U.N.-designated terrorist groups that we pay attention to. It is surely not the entire complete list because there are local groups with different places in the spectrum of extremism who are present in the environment as well who we have to pay attention to, and Libyans have to pay attention to. Some of them are purely domestic and I would distinguish those from the ones that operate in a transnational way.

But the four groups are: Islamic State. I have seen different numbers from the United States Government on how many are present. Prior to the Sirte offensive, the range in estimates were 3,000 to 6,500; I have seen numbers that many. Hundreds of Islamic State fighters have been killed in the Sirte fighting. Hundreds. Difficult to get an exact number but it is in that range. What are the numbers today? I don't think anyone knows. I would suspect they are at the lower end of that spectrum but there you would need to get briefings in closed session from people who are responsible for making those kinds of assessments.

In addition to Daesh, you have al-Qaeda in the Maghreb, which maintains an independent presence. They have been present in Benghazi, though at this point they are down to a sliver, a tiny sliver of territory in Benghazi. They have been basically eliminated there, and it is not clear how much longer they will hold the last block or two where they still have a presence. There is likely al-Qaeda cells elsewhere in the country.

There have been a couple of different groups calling themselves Ansar al-Sharia. One has been present in Darnah in the Far East. Another has been present in the far west of Libya, sometimes called Ansar al-Sharia Tunis. They have been responsible in significant part for attacks in Tunisia at the Bardo Museum and at the Sousse Beach area. So that is a third group.

A fourth group, Al-Mourabitoun, is present to some extent in Libya. They were Algerian-based originally, and they move around within countries to the west and south of Libya as well.

Those are the principal four groups. Beyond that, you get into constellations of militias with different types of ties. Some of whom disagree with and fight other Libyan militias and other Libyan military forces and that gets more complicated pretty quickly. The situation in Benghazi has been made complicated by the presence of some of those groups, along with people who are clearly Islamic State and people who are al-Qaeda in the Maghreb.

Mr. CHABOT. Thank you very much. My next question is this: There was a significant amount of criticism of the Bush administration for inadequately planning, shall we say, after the overthrow of Saddam in Iraq. Even after all that criticism, why did this administration fail to perhaps learn from that? And I think most people would agree there was a lack of planning for the power transition after Ghadafi and the situation that we have today. How could that happen and what can we learn in the future to avoid that type of thing from future administrations, including the current one, or the next administration, which will be coming in in about 2 months.

Mr. WINER. Mr. Chabot, it is an absolutely excellent core question and it is a question that deserves a lot of thought. I will do the best I can extemporaneously to respond.

In both Iraq and in Libya, you had dictatorships that had been in place for a very long time. When you have dictatorships, they tend to live in a bubble and not to have good political feedback mechanisms to have institutions function in ways other than by the command of the dictator.

So, in both cases, the institutions that were left following the military actions did not function in the absence of the authoritarian leader telling everybody what to do. They probably did not function tremendously well previously, but they certainly functioned very terribly afterward. So I think there needs to be a recognition any time one goes after a dictator that the societies, that the dictators have led for decades, are going to have underdeveloped political institutions.

In the case of Libya, there are technocratic institutions that functioned very well under Ghadafi and have functioned well since. The National Oil Corporation functioned very well to get oil pumped, to keep track of oil, and to handle all elements of Libyan oil production. Central Bank, technically, is capable of functioning to move money for salaries, to be able to follow budgets and make payments in that way similarly, and to operate as other central banks do. The National Telecommunications and Postal Service, same kind of technical capacity.

But political institutions, not so much. In politics, you have different people whose view is: I am the one who should decide, not that gentleman or woman over there. And no accepted agreed-upon mechanism for power sharing. So there have been disagreements pretty much nonstop on how to share power, how to deliver services at the local level, how to make the key decisions to move ahead. Constant negotiations and efforts to get alignment among the different geographies, geographical regions, the different tribes, the different cities, as well as the different political parties and ideologies. So it has made for a very, very difficult transition for Libya, as it did for Iraq.

So I think anytime one is going to engage in trying to undertake an intervention in another country, you have to do so with a lot of humility, with an appreciation of risk and of uncertainty, and with constant review before, while you're doing it, and afterward to be able to correct course as you go. You also need alignment from neighbors. If you have neighbors with different visions on the future engaging in a country, different regional players, for example, you can wind up with different domestic groups being backed by different regional forces, and, thereby, believing that they are going to be victorious as a result of having their patron. So it has been critical, in the case of Libya, to try and get regional players aligned with one another in support of a joint and unified solution, that is what we have been working on.

Mr. CHABOT. Thank you. My time has expired.

The gentleman from California, Mr. Cook, is recognized for 5 minutes.

Mr. COOK. Thank you, Mr. Chair. By the way, thank you very much for your patience with everything that is going on today. I wanted to just get your thoughts on the relationship with Egypt and the el-Sisi government. A number of years ago, going way back, the relationship between Libya and Egypt was strained, to say the least. I know that Egypt is concerned with the Sinai and its own economic development, but it would seem that Egypt could have a tremendous influence in that region there going back to historic times. Do you have any comments or thoughts on that?

Mr. WINER. Sure. Egypt is a tremendously important actor in relationship to Libya. It has a long-shared border, a long-shared history, and Egyptian officials very much want to see a stable and secure Libya. The question for the United States as we work closely with Egypt—and we work closely with literally all of Libya's neighbors across the Mediterranean, as well as on land, and with other regional players—is what is going to produce stability and security for the long term?

As I mentioned in my testimony, we are convinced that you have to have a viable national government as well as viable national security forces working together in a way that is sustainable. That means a government that is inclusive—it can't just be a government from the east or representing Easterners, for example—it has to include people from Misurata, people from Tripoli, people from the south.

The United States and Egypt talk about Libya all the time; I have been to Cairo, I don't know how many times in recent months, meeting with very senior officials. And to date, we have been able to achieve alignments in supporting the Libyan Political Agreement, in a series of U.N. Security Council resolutions, and even on stopping flows of illicit oil when they have happened. We have had cooperation and integration.

There are differences in perspective in some areas. Egypt wants to see a very strong Libyan army, we want to see a strong Libyan army too. I think our focus has been on how you get that integrated across the whole country in a way that is under civilian rule, civilian control, but also maintains the ability to do its job properly. We continue to work with them on that.

Mr. COOK. Thank you. I yield back.

Mr. CHABOT. The gentleman yields back.

The gentleman from Florida, Mr. DeSantis, didn't I hear that you just had an addition to your family?

Mr. DESANTIS. That is right.

Mr. CHABOT. A little girl?

Mr. DESANTIS. It is a little girl. A bundle of joy.

Mr. CHABOT. Congratulations.

Mr. DESANTIS. Oh, no, it is tremendous. Thank you so much.

You mentioned Ansar al-Sharia, they were widely regarded as perpetrating the Benghazi attacks. I know that the administration has indicted one individual from that. Has there been any other efforts made or actions taken to hold anyone else accountable who was involved with those attacks?

Mr. WINER. The FBI has active engagement in trying to bring the perpetrators of those attacks to justice. The Department of State and every element of the Obama administration, whenever there is an opportunity to try and advance those investigations, work away at it. One of the most important things to me, as special envoy, when we worked on the formation of the Government of National Accord was being able to talk to the new members of the presidency council about this case and to say how much it matters to us. They said, It matters to us, Mr. Winer, at least as much as it matters to you. Libyans loved Chris Stevens, they knew Ambassador Stevens very well. The other three victims of that attack also require and deserve justice. The Libyans raise this issue with me when we are talking about other things, they want to see us back in the country and they want to see this episode brought to a close with justice. I have never heard any Libyan I have talked to take a different position. There is an emotional element to this that is important to the future of both countries, I thank you for raising it.

Mr. DESANTIS. And just judging by your response and mentioning the FBI, am I right to assume that the response is legal/investigatory rather than kinetic in conjunction with, say, the Department of Defense?

Mr. WINER. The FBI has had the lead on this issue since those attacks took place. I personally believe that if we have the ability to go after terrorists in Libya, or anywhere, who have been involved in the killing of Americans, that we should exercise that. In the case of Libya, this administration has done so on multiple occasions. We went after and killed ISIL's emir, who was located at that time in the eastern half of Libya's coastal region. We went after a group of terrorists in western Libya, a very, very successful attack that killed a number of them. And we should be prepared to do that when it meets the objective test of people who are threatening Americans or have killed Americans.

Mr. DESANTIS. Well, good. Well, I am glad to hear you say that. I think that is true and I think it has been a little frustrating with the Benghazi response just simply because we had identified a group, and I view that very much as an act of war. You know, the law enforcement component I get, but I think when that was done in the 1990s that probably wasn't as effective. I certainly support the other strike that you had mentioned, I think that those were absolutely justified.

Let me ask you this: Of the folks who are kind of on the ground in Libya, the various groups that the U.S. is working with, what are they seeking? Are they seeking just to put an end to a lot of the turmoil? Do they want a more democratic pluralistic society? Do they want a more Islamic-based society where you would have a Sharia-type system? What would you say are kind of in the mix?

Mr. WINER. Are you talking about the terrorist groups?

Mr. DESANTIS. No, no. I am talking about just groups that we are working with.

Mr. WINER. Oh, sure.

Mr. DESANTIS. What are their orientations?

Mr. WINER. First, I think most Libyans want to see a stable, prosperous, secure Libya. They want good lives, like people want in any other country in the world. So most people in the first instance, that is what they want. It is getting there that is so hard. Getting the leaders to negotiate with one another, compromise with one another to create a unified government based on reconciliation that can build trust by performing. That is what most Libyans, I believe, want. And the many, many, many groups of Libyans, different Libyan leaders I talk to, profess to want the same thing. Libyans that we are working with on the battle over Sirte did not like and did not want to be threatened by a foreign brutal repellent ideology and organization that was milking Libyan resources to accrete power and to stifle all alternatives. They felt very strongly that that needed to be stopped.

In Benghazi, prior to the Libyan National Army commanded by General Haftar coming in, there were assassinations in civil society that were really significantly affecting the ability of ordinary people to live. The goal is to get the forces that we have supported in the west, the forces that General Haftar has brought together in the east, and other forces, including those being put together in Tripoli now from people who used to work for the Libyan Army in the past, together to form an integrated military that is non-ideological, that is technocratic, that is impartial and neutral, nonpolitical, whose goal is to stabilize Libya and make the country safe for people to carry out their business and live normal, good lives in safety. A political agreement is going to be necessary to further political negotiations and discussions within the framework of the Skhirat agreement is going to be necessary to get there, we believe. And we have been working on that intensively and will continue to.

Mr. DESANTIS. So is that more of an Egyptian model, then, you are looking forward with how their military has operated through the years?

Mr. CHABOT. The gentleman's time has expired. But you can go ahead and answer the question.

Mr. WINER. Yes, sir. I wouldn't call it an Egyptian model. It needs to be a Libyan model. Libyans will need to have, we believe, a joint defense leadership at the top in some way. There can be one person who is in the lead and others as part of it, but it is going to need to be joint because it needs to knit the country together. You know, Egypt has had a strong, strong leadership out of Cairo for thousands of years, for a long, long time, out of one city. Long tradition in the 20th century of Egyptian military. Libya has a more geographically diverse population, and it is going to need to be something that brings people together.

Mr. CHABOT. The gentleman's time has expired.

The gentleman from Florida, Mr. Yoho, is recognized for 5 minutes.

Mr. YOHO. Thank you, Mr. Chairman. I appreciate you being here, and sorry for the delay. You were talking about the flow of oil; the operation of it, the production, and the sale operated well under Ghadafi, is that right?

Mr. WINER. Yes, sir.

Mr. Yoho. All right. And now it is kind of happenstance? It is not working as well?

Mr. Winer. What has happened, in essence, is the different Libyan factions have shut down oil production as a means of trying to get their way. You could call it extortion, if you wanted to, in some cases but, essentially, they have simply turned off the spigots. Libyan oil flows from fields to pipes to terminals.

Mr. Yoho. Right.

Mr. Winer. So you can shut it off at the terminal, you can shut it off at the pipe, you can shut it off at the oil field.

Mr. Yoho. And then you were talking about we need to have a viable national government, an inclusive government. Is that possible when you have a tribal mentality, or a country with a tribal mentality versus a strong arm of a leader like a Ghadafi or a Hussein in Iraq? Is that possible in that kind of a country with that kind of mentality?

Mr. Winer. The aftermath of dictatorship is very hard on people almost anywhere it happens. In the case of Libya, Libyans need to come together to form a government that represents——

Mr. Yoho. Well, that is what I am asking. Is that possible? We have seen this story played out in Afghanistan and Iraq, and what I see is America trying to correct a wrong from the no-fly zone that we know was a mistake; a terrible mistake, and we almost repeated this again in Syria. Here we are entangled in another Middle Eastern country with not a quick resolve and I just want to see what your thoughts are on how do we get through this? And as a unity government, and I know that would be the ideal situation, but how feasible is that and how realistic is that?

Mr. Winer. I believe that Libyans don't like people from other countries telling them what to do.

Mr. Yoho. I agree.

Mr. Winer. And they don't much like other Libyans telling them what to do. But they would rather be in the end, working things out among other Libyans than having foreigners in charge. One of the reasons the Islamic State has been pushed out of geographic control so quickly, in the scheme of things, is because Libyans, even the extremists in the east who invited them into Darnah, started saying: We don't want them telling us what to do. We don't want those people out of Iraq or Syria telling us what to do. We are going to be extremists, we will be local extremists; we don't like other people telling us what to do.

Mr. Yoho. Well, and that brings up another point then. If ISIS got a foothold in there because of the no-fly zone, because of the failed state, and now that we are trying to side with different militias to defeat ISIS, are we not going to create the same thing that we did in Afghanistan?

Mr. Winer. Our goal is not to side with any militia. It is to help Libyans get together to form unified forces that are professional, impartial, neutral.

Mr. Yoho. Is that possible though?

Mr. Winer. Yes, I think it is possible. Sometimes things that are hard are still possible.

Mr. Yoho. I agree.

Mr. WINER. Just because something is hard does not mean it is impossible.

Mr. YOHO. No, I agree with that.

Mr. WINER. It was considered to be really hard to create a political framework in 2015 to try and bring the country together. Ultimately, we were able to work with other countries, countries with very different takes and perspectives on the Libyan issue throughout the region—Middle Eastern region and throughout North Africa—were able to say: Yes, we agree, this is the way forward. As well as western European countries, the United States, and the P5 and the U.N. Security Council. We had an awful lot of Libyans aboard, too. The goal now is to try and see if we can continue to get Libyans together, to find further solutions to implement that long enough to then get a referendum on a constitution and elections in place, so that you can have the country then move forward on that basis, with unified national institutions. If the country winds up breaking up into pieces, it is going to be very bad for Libyans and it is not going to be good for anybody else.

Mr. YOHO. Do you see a strong person that could be elected in there that people would unify right now? Or do you see it still going through the struggling—somebody trying to vie for the power, so that they are the person that can be elected? Or are they going to just kind of take the country over through force?

Mr. WINER. We do not believe that any Libyan can bring the country together through force. We just don't believe it. We look at it and say: Is it possible? Conclude it is not going to work. It will bring other Libyans into play against it if anyone tries to do that, and our partners and working on Libya, international partners, pretty much, conclude the same thing. It is going to be a process of getting there; promoting alignment, getting people to work with one another, preventing the efforts to commandeer resources, that is the ongoing work. And it is going to need to continue with some intensity for the foreseeable future.

Mr. YOHO. I appreciate it. Thank you.

Mr. CHABOT. Thank you. The gentleman's time has expired.

The gentleman from Wisconsin, Mr. Ribble, is recognized for 5 minutes.

Mr. RIBBLE. Good afternoon, I guess.

Mr. WINER. Yes, sir.

Mr. RIBBLE. It is good to have you here. I want to go back to the economy, to some of the very early statements you made. Because I think ultimately, I couldn't agree more with you when you talk about that the citizens want an economy that functions, they want families that are safe, they want their children to do well. They really want all the same things that families around the world want. Can you share with us a little bit of your perspective of what the Libyan economy looked like under Ghadafi——

Mr. WINER. Sure.

Mr. RIBBLE [continuing]. And what it looks like today? You talked a bit about oil, but what are the other economic drivers in the country? And then also talk to us about what those obstacles are. Are they religious? Is it a Sunni/Shia battle? Is it economic? Is it just dispirit——

Mr. WINER. Yes, sir.

Mr. RIBBLE. So just kind of take us through what you see the economic——

Mr. WINER. Thank you for another great question. Ghadafi's strength and weakness was building the Libyan economy on oil and almost exclusively oil. There is essentially no revenue to the government meaningfully other than oil. There are small amounts from telecommunications payments, that kind of thing, postal payments, some excise taxes but it is basically oil. So when the price of oil was high, Libya under Ghadafi socked the money away. When the price of oil was lower, it managed.

In the first days after the revolution, Libya continued to pump as much oil as it ever did. They started fighting with one another, oil production went down. They then resolved things for a while, oil production went up to where it had been pre-Ghadafi again. So the reason why oil is not being pumped at an adequate level is political. It is not technical. It is not due to deterioration of the system, though Islamic State did damage some infrastructure that needs to be repaired, if they had complete political agreement, maybe they could get up to 1.2 or 1.3 million barrels a day instead of 1.6. They would be in excellent shape with that. So it is the failure to reach political agreements that is creating the problems. It is this pattern of extortion, holdups, people refusing to allow oil to be pumped for political reasons. That is what has to stop. It is a cancer threatening Libya's future when people shut down the oil.

Then the money from the oil has to be distributed in ways that ordinary Libyans throughout the country say: Our city, our town, our tribe, our people, our region, are being taken care of. Ghadafi was good at that; he wasn't necessarily fair, he didn't distribute it in a way that everybody else would have distributed it, but there was free education, there was low-cost health care, low cost utilities. So while there were haves and have-nots that were substantial and that played a part in the revolution, I believe, he basically had his Ghadafi system down. Without him acting as the leader, that system is broken down and you have these people shutting down the oil, which he never would have permitted. They need to get the oil pumped. There is no solution near-term other than getting oil pumped so they can generate the revenues they need to then distribute it by political agreement. So what we are working on right now, in addition to urging Libyans to allow oil to be pumped, and right now, there is 440,000 barrels a day that could be pumped from the west by a small number of people saying yes——

Mr. RIBBLE. Is there an effective telecommunications system in the country where citizens can communicate easily through the Internet and cell phones?

Mr. WINER. Yes. It is not as robust as it needs to be because there hasn't been investment in it in the last 5 years, and Islamic State, at various times, tried cutting the cords, as it were, shutting down elements of it, but it still exists. It could be stronger and needs to be stronger.

Mr. RIBBLE. Because it is important economically for the people to communicate.

Mr. WINER. Yeah. Libya needs to diversify beyond oil, but first it needs to turn the oil on, agree on budgets, agree on fiscal and monetary policy in light of current conditions, and reach further political agreements that would strengthen and build confidence among the Libyan people, thus shutting off the losses due to the parallel or black market. We are working closely with the U.S. Department of Treasury and with Libyans in trying to promote their agreement on those issues, as well as with IMF and the World Bank.

Mr. RIBBLE. One final question. In hindsight, and I recognize hindsight is generally 20/20, what should the U.S. have done differently, if anything? Did we learn anything there?

Mr. WINER. As I mentioned before, and I will repeat this core point, anytime that you go into a country that has been run by a dictator, the aftermath could be very complicated because that is a particular type of system. Getting to a system that is more pluralistic and more representative, which is essential for countries to be sustainable. There is a reason why dictators fall, eventually their systems rot and they no longer meet the needs of their people and they can't maintain control. When you do that, you have to go in with humility, persistence, and commitment, you have to know a lot, listen a lot, be prepared to revise your initial thinking, consult with other people, and recognize that it can be a bunch of years.

I worked on issues in the Americas in the 1990s in the Clinton years. My rule of thumb used to be that after a civil war or the fall of a dictatorship or anything of that nature, and military or security forces becoming discredited, no longer being in place, you have to think about a decade for rebuilding, not a year or 2 years, but a decade. That is not a very perfect rule but it is order of magnitude what I have seen now over decades of being in this work. The other line I sometimes use is: Don't try to do in Baghdad what you would never dare try to do in Baltimore, because you know it wouldn't work if you tried to do it in Baltimore. So I use the word again, ''humility.'' Governance is hard and the further away you are from a society, the harder it is. You can still help by being very attuned to a society and consulting and learning but it is difficult, painstaking work that takes time.

Mr. CHABOT. The gentleman's time has expired. Thank the gentleman.

We want to thank you, Mr. Winer, for you testimony here this morning and now this afternoon. In my Democratic colleagues' defense, their absence is not due to a lack of interest, but they had leadership elections, which apparently went a little longer than they anticipated. So their absence, of course, is excused.

We want to thank everyone for being here. Thank you for your testimony. Members will have 5 legislative days to submit statements or questions or to extend their remarks. And if there is no further business to come before the committee, we are adjourned. Thank you very much.

[Whereupon, at 12:11 p.m., the subcommittees were adjourned.]

APPENDIX

MATERIAL SUBMITTED FOR THE RECORD

JOINT SUBCOMMITTEE HEARING NOTICE
COMMITTEE ON FOREIGN AFFAIRS
U.S. HOUSE OF REPRESENTATIVES
WASHINGTON, DC 20515-6128

Subcommittee on the Middle East and North Africa
Ileana Ros-Lehtinen (R-FL), Chairman

Subcommittee on Terrorism, Nonproliferation, and Trade
Ted Poe (R-TX), Chairman

November 29, 2016

TO: MEMBERS OF THE COMMITTEE ON FOREIGN AFFAIRS

You are respectfully requested to attend an OPEN hearing of the Committee on Foreign Affairs, to be held jointly by the Subcommittee on the Middle East and North Africa and the Subcommittee on Terrorism, Nonproliferation, and Trade in Room 2172 of the Rayburn House Office Building (and available live on the Committee website at http://www.ForeignAffairs.house.gov):

DATE: Wednesday, November 30, 2016

TIME: 10:30 a.m.

SUBJECT: Libya Five Years After Ghadafi

WITNESSES: Mr. Jonathan Winer
Special Envoy for Libya
Bureau of Near Eastern Affairs
U.S. Department of State

By Direction of the Chairman

The Committee on Foreign Affairs seeks to make its facilities accessible to persons with disabilities. If you are in need of special accommodations, please call 202/225-5021 at least four business days in advance of the event, whenever practicable. Questions with regard to special accommodations in general (including availability of Committee materials in alternative formats and assistive listening devices) may be directed to the Committee.

COMMITTEE ON FOREIGN AFFAIRS

MINUTES OF SUBCOMMITTEE ON *Middle East and North Africa/ Terrorism, Nonproliferation and Trade* HEARING

Day **Wednesday** Date *November 30th, 2016* Room _____ *2172* _____

Starting Time *11:27 am* Ending Time *12:12 pm*

Recesses |_____| (____to ____) (____to ____) (____to ____) (____to ____) (____to ____) (____to ____)

Presiding Member(s)

Chairman Ileana Ros-Lehtinen, Representative Steve Chabot

Check all of the following that apply:

Open Session ✓   Electronically Recorded (taped) ✓
Executive (closed) Session ☐   Stenographic Record ✓
Televised ☐

TITLE OF HEARING:

Libya: Five Years After Ghadafi

SUBCOMMITTEE MEMBERS PRESENT:

MENA- Chairman Ileana Ros-Lehtinen, Representatives Steve Chabot, Ted Yoho, Ron DeSantis
TNT- Representatives Reid Ribble, Paul Cook, Scott Perry

NON-SUBCOMMITTEE MEMBERS PRESENT: *(Mark with an * if they are not members of full committee.)*

HEARING WITNESSES: Same as meeting notice attached? Yes ✓ No ☐
(If "no", please list below and include title, agency, department, or organization.)

STATEMENTS FOR THE RECORD: *(List any statements submitted for the record.)*

Subcommittee on Terrorism, Nonproliferation, and Trade and Chairman Ted Poe's Opening Statement
Subcommittee on the Middle East and North Africa Ranking Member Theodore Deutch Statement
Representative Gerald Connolly Statement

TIME SCHEDULED TO RECONVENE _____
or
TIME ADJOURNED *12:12 p.m.*

_____
Subcommittee Staff Associate

Opening Statement
Chairman Ileana Ros-Lehtinen
Joint MENA/TNT Hearing: Libya: Five Years After Ghadafi
Wednesday, November 30, 2016, 10:00 a.m.; 2172 Rayburn

The Subcommittees will come to order.

After recognizing myself, Ranking Member Deutch, and Ranking Member Keating for 5 minutes each for our opening statements, I will then recognize other Members seeking recognition for 1 minute.

We will then hear from our witness and without objection, the witness's prepared statement will be made part of the record and Members may have 5 days to insert statements and questions for the record, subject to the length limitations in the rules.

Before beginning my opening statement, I'd first like to take a moment to acknowledge the other Chairman of this joint subcommittee hearing, Judge Poe.

Judge Poe could not be here with us this morning as he continues to undergo treatment for leukemia, and I know all of our thoughts and prayers are with him as he fights this terrible disease.

I have his opening statement here and without objection, it will be made part of the record.

The Chair now recognizes herself for five minutes.

December 17th marks the one year anniversary of the Libyan Political Agreement, making this an opportune time to review the administration's policy in Libya. When this administration first participated in the intervention in Libya in 2011, many of us expressed concern with the administration's lack of clearly articulated objectives, a post-intervention plan, or even an explanation about how it fit U.S. national security interests. Many of our worst fears have come to fruition, as more than five years after Ghadafi's death; Libya is embroiled in a civil war that shows no sign of abatement.

If anything, it has only gotten worse since the UN-brokered agreement. Libya is more politically divided than ever, its economy is in freefall, and terrorist groups and criminals continue to exploit the power vacuum. Multiple governing entities and their allied militias and armed forces vie for power, while the UN-backed unity government, known as the Government of National Accord, remains unable to provide basic security and services to the Libyan people. Criminals and terrorist groups, including ISIS, al-Qaeda and others, take advantage of the chaos, securing their own territory and using Libya as a launching point for smuggling, human trafficking, and terror attacks – endangering Libya's neighbors like Egypt and Tunisia.

Libya is now the main transit point for migrants trying to reach Europe, and with little border security or governance, many are rightly concerned by the potential of terrorists reaching our own shores. While reports say that forces are close to retaking Sirte from ISIS, we should not allow this news to disguise the reality: ISIS's presence in Libya is far from being eliminated. ISIS, al-Qaeda, and Ansar al-Sharia, the group responsible for the 2012 Benghazi attack, as well as others, all continue to maintain cells throughout the country.

In a positive development, I was relieved to see the announcement last month that the Organization for the Prohibition of Chemical Weapons was able to remove Libya's remaining chemical weapons precursors. Another welcome development, if accurate, is the reported killing by French airstrikes of the Algerian jihadist known as the "one-eyed terrorist." He is said to be responsible for organizing terrorist attacks in Libya, Algeria, Mali, and elsewhere, and had funneled millions of dollars to al-Qaeda.

France's airstrikes highlight the stakes that many outside actors have in Libya. Russia, Egypt, Saudi Arabia, the UAE, and others continue to support Khalifa Haftar, the former Libyan National Army general who recently claimed victory in Benghazi and who was just in Moscow discussing Russian military assistance.
Reports indicate that at least four different countries have Special Forces on the ground in Libya right now, including our own, and, in some cases, are assisting forces on both sides of Libya's civil war.

It also worth noting that in recent months Haftar has seized many of the ports in Libya's oil crescent – Libya's main source of revenue. With additional violence on the horizon, potentially between eastern and western forces, Haftar's role must be addressed in Libya's political dialogue – a dialogue that should come sooner rather than later.

Since the unity government took up residence in Tripoli in March, it has struggled to provide the kind of basic services and security that could engender the support it needs to consolidate power. And as long as it keeps struggling in the west while its rival governing entities and security forces keep operating and making gains in the east, any chance that the current peace process had at succeeding will continue to be undermined.

As we approach the one year anniversary of the Libyan Political Agreement, it is clear that the status quo in Libya is unsustainable and that there must be a new and revitalized attempt at reconciling all Libyan stakeholders. I look forward to hearing from our witness exactly how the administration is working to help get that peace process back on track, the status of our counterterrorism operations against ISIS and others, and what kind of changes to our Libya policy and assistance we should expect moving forward.

Opening Statement Chairman Ted Poe
Joint TNT & MENA Subcommittee Hearing "Libya Five Years After Ghadafi"
11/30/2016

For six months, the U.S.-backed troops of the interim Libyan Government of National Accord has been fighting street by street to retake the ISIS stronghold of Sirte on the Libyan coast. ISIS seized control of the city in early 2015 and extended its control along about 155 miles of Libya's coastline. That means that ISIS wields its influence over a territory roughly the distance from Houston to San Antonio. How did the US get here? How did Libya become an incubator for all stripes of terrorists?

In 2008, U.S. military leaders were calling Libya a top U.S. ally in combating international terrorism. Ghadafi realized that his regime was the target of terrorism, and he changed course from supporting terrorists in the 1980s to siding with the US against the terrorist threat. However, in 2011, in the midst of a rebellion against the Ghadafi regime, the US decided to intervene and establish a no-fly zone to aid the Libyan rebels. Under the safety of the no-fly zone the US imposed, Islamist terrorist groups long subdued under Ghadafi's regime sprung up and amassed weapons, training, and military training.

Ghadafi was ultimately killed in October 2011. Within days, NATO and U.S. forces packed up and left Libya to its own devices. America's only Libya policy at the time was to remove Ghadafi – there was little planning regarding what to do the day after. The US opened the Pandora's box and looked away.

Almost immediately after Ghadafi's ouster, Libya spiraled into chaos. Long simmering political, regional, and ethnic divisions suddenly emerged and set Libya on a path towards disaster. The country has never recovered. Even the Administration has admitted its role Libya's failure. Earlier this year, the President admitted that there was no plan for post-Ghadafi Libya, describing it as his biggest regret as President.

Libya has become a regional and international security threat due to this Administration's lack of planning. ISIS and al-Qaeda are the main beneficiaries. Al-Qaeda's Libyan affiliate, Ansar al-Shariah, emerged shortly after Ghadafi's death and has since become deeply entrenched in the country. They have successfully filled the void the US helped create by providing social services – building schools and providing medical care. But they did not stop there. They recruited, armed, and trained terrorist fighters intent on carrying out the group's ultimate goal: imposing Islamic law on the country. Ansar al-Shariah fighters were among those who ultimately attacked the U.S.

diplomatic compound in Benghazi in 2012, killing Ambassador Christopher Stevens and three of his colleagues.

Since then, things have gotten worse. ISIS announced the establishment of a Libyan affiliate at the end of 2014 and soon began consolidating its power around Sirte and expanding east, west, and south. America should not fool itself into believing that once Sirte is liberated the ISIS threat is over. For close to a year now, ISIS has been redirecting recruits and even senior leaders to Libya. It has been laying the seeds for what many have called a "fallback Caliphate," where it could retreat to in case it is pushed out of Syria and Iraq.

Pentagon estimates from earlier this year suggested that the group's ranks in Libya have swelled to nearly 7,000 fighters. Liberating Sirte will simply transform the ISIS threat in Libya from a concentrated one to a dispersed one. They have fanned out throughout the country and will continue to exploit the political mess in Libya. Libya will unfortunately remain a terrorist foothold for years to come. This is the legacy of the current Administration in North Africa.

The mess the US have left there has spread throughout the region. It endangers Egyptian allies to the east, and the weapons unleashed with Ghadafi's fall have fueled terrorism in places like Syria, Nigeria, and the Sinai Peninsula bordering Israel. The United States' airstrike campaign in support of the Libyan forces retaking Sirte is only a small step.

Until the US can devise a truly comprehensive long-term strategy to stabilize Libya and defeat the terrorist groups hiding there, Libya will continue to threaten regional and international security. Treating the symptoms while ignoring the underlying disease will not solve the problem. The US forcibly overthrew a regime in Libya, creating chaos that led to a failed state where terrorists flourished and thousands of Libyans died. The US now has a responsibility to work towards a stabilizing solution in Libya. Going forward, the US should be much more cautious before it helps overthrow another regime.

Ranking Member Ted Deutch Opening Statement
MENA Hearing "Libya Five Years After Ghadafi"
November 30, 2016

Thank you, Madam Chairman for convening today's hearing. I'd also like to send my thoughts and prayers to Chairman Poe. Thanks to Special Envoy Winer for your service and for appearing today. I am pleased to have the opportunity to focus some attention on the political and security situation in Libya.

While the US and our allies have been focused on combatting ISIS in Iraq and Syria and on ending the carnage of the Syrian conflict, Libya has plunged into chaos with little attention from the international community.

Five years after the fall of Muammar Ghadafi's 40 year dictatorship, Libya has been unable to stabilize its government or security situation. Since the elected House of Representatives was challenged by the interim General National Congress in 2014, the country has been governed by competing factions. A UN-mediated process to end this stalemate resulted in what seemed to be a hopeful framework for a unity government. By early 2016, plans were in place for the formation of a Government of National Accord. The GNA was designed to bring together House of Representatives as a legislative power in partnership with a State Council made up of former GNC members. A nine-member Presidency Council would have national security and economic executive powers. The Council would have representation from various factions of Libyan society. While the GNA gained initial support from the House of Representatives, that support has slowly dwindled culminating in an August vote of no confidence in the new government. Complicating the formation of a new governance structure has been the ever-shifting military alliances among Libya's leaders.

In 2014, General Haftar's forces began to fight Islamic extremist elements trying to take hold in Libya. Haftar steadily gained the support of many HOR members and of powerful neighbors like Egypt. Many Haftar aligned HOR members are opposed to the transfer of military powers to the eventual Presidency Council. As ISIS gained a greater foothold in Libya, pro-GNA forces have also been battling to drive ISIS from their foothold in Sirte. In August the US launched Operation Odyssey Lightening to provide air support to forces battling ISIS. According to reports over the past month, Libyan forces are seeing success driving ISIS from Sirte; but, as the Pentagon stated just weeks ago, ISIS militants appear to be "fighting to the death." Despite the desire and success of most pro-government factions to drive ISIS and other extremists from Libya, this has not brought the groups any closer to completing the formation of the unity government.

While the United States has been steadily assisting Libya in a military and counterterrorism capacity, what further pressure can be exerted by the US and our allies to push the unity government forward?

Libya's economy has suffered dramatically as a result of the security situation. Oil production had been on the decline and was further complicated by General Haftar's seizure of four major oil production facilities. Economic instability has no doubt driven political instability. The United Nations Security Council has twice affirmed that control over oil production belongs in the hands of the GNA, and that proceeds from oil production belong to the country. UN Security Council resolution 2278 states that UN member states should assist in preventing oil exports that are not authorized by the GNA through July 2017 and requested that the GNA notify the Council "as soon as it exercises sole and effective oversight over the National Oil Corporation and the Central Bank of Libya." How successfully can this be implemented? And if efforts are made to stabilize Libya's oil production, what impact could this have on moving the political process forward?

Since the fall of Ghadafi, we have discussed the dangers posed by a Libya in chaos. We have seen ISIS try to use Libya as a training ground and staging ground for attacks in North Africa. We have seen the migrant crisis explode from Libya's shores, in fact just this morning *The Washington Post* detailed a surge in migration from Libya to Italy. We know too well what happens to a restless youth population that does not see any prospects for economic opportunity and prosperity. All of this leads us to the central question of today's hearing: given the ever changing security and political landscape, how is US policy toward Libya evolving?

The US embassy has been operating out of Malta since 2014. How is the lack of US personnel on the ground in Libya affecting our ability to respond to the needs of Libyan society and to shape and aid the political transition? In addition, I am concerned that the longer Libya goes without a stable government, we risk losing a partner that the US can reliably work with on mutual security objectives.

The consequences of a failed Libyan state would be dire on international and US security. After so many years under repressive rule, the people of Libya deserve stability and a brighter future.

I look forward to getting the chance to address the issues I've raised this morning with you, Special Envoy Winer.

Statement for the Record
Submitted by Mr. Connolly of Virginia

It has been more than two years since the Subcommittee last held a hearing on Libya. Sadly, the situation on the ground has not materially improved, and the country remains embroiled in conflict. Several militant groups continue to operate with impunity, and rival political factions have been unable to form a stable and united national government. Since 2014, the Islamic State of Iraq and the Levant (ISIL) has established and expanded a branch of its organization in three provinces in Libya, threatening not only territorial integrity, but also energy infrastructure vital to the nation's economy. Given President-elect Donald Trump's starkly contrasting statements on U.S. policy toward Libya throughout the campaign, it is difficult to analyze the way forward.

Following the June 2014 elections, the House of Representatives (HOR) and a group of military officers aligned with the Libyan National Army (LNA) led by retired General Khalifa Haftar have established an internationally recognized government in eastern Libya and have waged an aggressive campaign against a range of Islamist forces. Meanwhile, in western Libya, remnants of the former General National Congress (GNC) have so far refused to recognize the HOR's legitimacy.

In late 2015, the United Nations facilitated a dialogue to establish an interim Government of National Accord (GNA) tasked with overseeing Libya's transition. The United States and our European partners recognize the GNA as Libya's best hope for peace and stability, and have supported its development accordingly. In June, the U.N. Security Council extended the U.N. Support Mission in Libya through December and reiterated its support for the GNA as the sole legitimate Government of Libya. However, not all governing entities in Libya have signed onto the GNA, and questions remain over unified political leadership and military command, national finances, and control of oil infrastructure. Such international backing has led some Libyan contingents to describe GNA leaders as "foreign-imposed interlopers." HOR members aligned with General Haftar take specific issue with recognizing the GNA Presidency Council as the legitimate leaders of Libya's armed forces.

In August 2016, GNA Prime Minister-designate Fayez al Sarraj requested an expansion of U.S. military operations against the Libyan branch of ISIL. U.S.-supported Libyan forces are currently battling ISIL fighters in the coastal city of Sirte, which has been under the terrorist group's control since mid-2015. While anti-ISIL fighters have greatly reduced ISIL's control of the city, they have been plagued by significant casualties and limited resources, and the campaign to eliminate ISIL's presence in the city is expected to drag on for months. Unfortunately, ISIL is not the only transnational jihadist threat in Libya. Ansar al Sharia and other radical jihadist and secular militia groups continue to battle for regional control.

Libya's ongoing conflict and weak governance have opened up the country to a host of ancillary problems, including human trafficking; illegal migration; institutional rivalries; as well as food, fuel, and power shortages.

Unfortunately, President-elect Donald Trump's comments on Libya offer little clarity on the new Administration's path forward. President-elect Trump has both emphatically supported and ardently opposed U.S. military intervention in Libya. Prior to Qadhafi's removal, Trump called for a "surgical" knockout of the dictator "on a humanitarian basis" to save the lives of those he threatened to massacre. Then during the presidential campaign, Trump claimed that "we'd be so much better off if Qadhafi were in charge right now." I am interested in the conversations the current Administration has had with President-elect Trump's transition team regarding his administration's approach to fragile states in general and Libya in particular. Clarity on this matter is needed desperately.

I look forward to a discussion on how the United States, in conjunction with our international and Libyan partners, plans to support compromise and demobilization among Libya's rival factions and root out transnational terrorist threats including ISIL. Ensuring a peaceful resolution and democratic governance will be an essential foundation to begin to address the many obstacles impeding Libya's progress. But let's be clear: the road ahead is a treacherous one lacking easy options for the United States.

Questions for the Record Submitted to
U.S. Special Envoy for Libya Jonathan M. Winer by
Representative Ros-Lehtinen
House Foreign Affairs Committee
Sub-Committees on the Middle East & North Africa and
Terrorism, Nonproliferation & Trade
November 30, 2016

Question:

Since the Government of National Accord set itself up in Tripoli in March, it has struggled to provide basic services to the Libyan people as many Libyans continue to deal with fuel, food, power, and cash shortages. The price of goods has skyrocketed as the rate of the dollar to the Libyan dinar has surged in recent weeks. How is the government responding to these challenges and what kind of assistance is the U.S. providing to the GNA in order to prevent economic collapse?

Answer:

To restore Libya's economy and ensure Libya's resources benefit all its people, the country needs a unified government working with the technocratic Central Bank of Libya (CBL) and National Oil Corporation (NOC) in Tripoli. This has been a central component of our diplomatic engagement.

We helped lay groundwork for this one year ago in the UN Security Council. Security Council resolution 2259 called on the Government of National Accord (GNA) to protect the integrity and unity of the CBL and NOC and on the CBL and NOC to accept, in turn, the GNA's authority. As the GNA was preparing to seat itself in Tripoli, we fostered contact between the government and leaders of the economic institutions to ensure they worked together to facilitate a successful transition. And since then, we have continued to encourage the GNA and the economic institutions to work aggressively to address Libya's serious, ongoing economic challenges, most recently in October and November by helping to organize high-level economic dialogue meetings in London and Rome. The Libyans face critical economic decisions that ultimately only they can make, but the United States has provided strong, consistent diplomatic support.

The U.S. Department of Treasury and USAID have provided assistance to the CBL and Finance Ministries on public financial management and on applying necessary controls to address counterterror finance concerns. The Department of Treasury has stressed the importance of Libya continuing to engage with the IMF and World Bank to develop effective policy responses for its economic challenges. USAID has embedded two advisors in the Ministry of Planning to provide technical assistance on macroeconomic and fiscal issues. USAID has provided advisors for short- and medium-term solutions, including an assessment of the electricity sector for the General Electric Company of Libya (GECOL). USAID also works with local partners to support tangible, visible community improvements and delivery of services in order to enable GNA ministries and local governance bodies to demonstrate action to their constituencies. To ensure these gains are sustainable USAID has worked with Ministry of Local Governance (MoLG) and municipalities to assist in building capacity for revenue generation, budget planning, budget execution, and procurement at the municipal level. The United States has also worked closely with the international community and Prime Minister Fayez al-Sarraj's government to prevent illicit oil shipments. Oil sales by anyone other than the Tripoli-based National Oil Corporation (NOC), under the GNA's supervision, would seriously damage the country's economy, threaten its unity, and likely fuel resource-based civil conflict. In April, the vessel "Distya Ameya" attempted to transport 650,000 barrels of Libyan crude outside traditional channels. After diplomatic outreach, led by the United States and international partners, the tanker turned around and returned the oil to the legitimate NOC. We continue to urge all Libyans to work together to restore Libya's oil production and exports, and stress the necessity for Libyan wealth to benefit all Libyans, as underlined by the Governing Principles of the Libyan Political Agreement (LPA) signed on December 17, 2015, as well as UN Security Council Resolution 2259 (2015).

Question:

In a joint communique signed in September, the United States and others declared that the GNA is the sole legitimate recipient of international security assistance. Yet many of these countries including France, which reportedly maintains a military base in Libya with the UAE, as well as Russia and others in the region, have been supporting the operations of Khalifa Haftar and his operations in the east. What are these countries' goals in supporting Haftar and how does their support for Haftar complicate efforts to assist the GNA? Is the United States supporting or cooperating with Haftar in any way? If so, how?

Answer:

The Government of National Accord (GNA) is Libya's sole legitimate recipient of international security assistance, as the international community made clear in the September 22 New York Joint Communique and the May 16 Vienna Communique on Libya. As stated in these communiques, all Libyan forces, including General Haftar and his "Libyan National Army," should unite under the GNA's civilian command. We have stressed to all sides publicly and privately on the imperative for Libya to build a national military force capable of securing and uniting the country. Disunity and lack of coordination among Libyan forces benefit only Da'esh and other violent extremists.

The United States abides by UNSCRs on Libya, including UNSCR 2259 of December 23, 2015, which forbids supporting parallel structures outside the Libyan GNA. The United States does not provide assistance to any military force in Libya except those that are under the GNA, and therefore the United States has not provided assistance to General Haftar or his forces. We cannot comment on other countries' goals, but the United States has worked with our partners to drive international community support for the Libyan Political Agreement and the GNA led by Prime Minister Fayez al-Sarraj.

Question:

How does the administration view Haftar's seizure and control of Libyan oil ports? How dependent is the GNA on oil revenue and is it possible for the economy to recover if the west and east aren't able to reconcile, increase oil production, and capture that revenue? How important is it to prevent the diversion of oil revenues from the Central Bank of Libya and the National Oil Corporation?

Answer:

As stated in a September 12 Joint Statement on Libya, the United States viewed General Haftar's move into the "Oil Crescent" with concern because of the risk of renewed civil conflict over resources and because it was a unilateral move that threatened to complicate ongoing efforts to achieve a negotiated compromise. In September, General Haftar's forces redeployed outside oil facilities, turning responsibility for direct security over to elements of the Petroleum Facilities Guard (PFG) and responsibility for technical operations to the Tripoli-based National Oil Corporation (NOC). These were positive steps, but it remains critical to Libya's economic stability that Libyan oil exports flow through the legitimate channels of the technocratic NOC, and oil revenues flow to the technocratic, Tripoli-based Central Bank of Libya (CBL), both of which are under the supervision of the Government of National Accord (GNA). The GNA will rely heavily on oil revenues for its operating expenses and to foster economic recovery.

We have stressed that it is critical for all sides in Libya to avoid further provocative actions and that there is no military solution to Libya's political challenges. We welcomed Prime Minister al-Sarraj's call for dialogue to reduce tensions in the "Oil Crescent" and foster reconciliation.

Question:

Some observers have suggested that, considering Libya's political divisions and recent violence between western and eastern forces, a unified Libya is becoming less viable. What can you tell us about the current violence between western and eastern forces in Libya's oil crescent and the potential for violence elsewhere? What would happen if Libya divides along regional lines?

Answer:

As of December 7, we are aware of clashes between "Libya National Army" (LNA) and anti-LNA forces west of oil ports in the Sirte Basin. We are concerned about these and other reports of violence across Libya, including in Sabha, Benghazi, and Tripoli, and we continue to urge all parties across Libya to exercise restraint. We reiterate our call for all parties to work together to create a safe, prosperous, and free Libya that provides for the needs of its people. We continue to urge all Libyans to put aside parochial interests for the national good of Libya and continue to implement the Libyan Political Agreement. Our strategy in Libya is founded on our assessment, which is shared with a great number of international partners, that the only hope for long-term stability and security in Libya is a unified national government. As the international community stated in the Joint Communique from the Secretary's September 22 meeting on Libya in New York, "We share the Libyan people's desire to transform Libya to become a secure, democratic, prosperous, and unified state, where state authority and the rule of law prevail. This can only be achieved peacefully through inclusive political dialogue and national reconciliation." A majority of Libyans support a united country. Dividing Libya along regional lines would lead to further civil conflict, fighting over resources, and instability.

Question:

While victory has been declared against ISIS in Sirte, reports indicate that ISIS continues to maintain cells throughout Libya. What can you tell us about ISIS' remaining presence? How many fighters do they have left?

Answer:

On December 6, the Government of National Accord (GNA) aligned forces reclaimed the last few Da'esh-controlled buildings in Sirte. We commend this progress. Prime Minister al-Sarraj's government and its aligned forces have been steadfast counterterrorism partners of the United States. At Prime Minister al-Sarraj's request, since August, we conducted nearly 500 air strikes against Da'esh in Sirte to support GNA-aligned forces on the ground. In the next phase of the fight, we will continue to cooperate closely with the GNA as it works to prevent Da'esh from finding safe haven anywhere in Libya.

There is more work to be done before Sirte can be deemed 'cleared and secure. The next challenge for the GNA and its aligned forces will be stabilizing Sirte after Da'esh's defeat. The United States and partner nations, in coordination with the UN Support Mission to Libya (UNSMIL) and UN Special Representative of the Secretary-General (SRSG) Martin Kobler, are working with the GNA to develop a plan to stabilize the city, including U.S.-funded programs for mine, unexploded ordnance, and improvised explosive device clearance.

Da'esh strength in Libya was once assessed to be approximately 5,000, but that is a number we constantly reassess. The Da'esh fighters in Sirte that were not killed have mostly moved to other Libyan towns or attempted to leave Libya altogether. Libya has joined the Global Coalition to Counter-ISIL and together with the 68 members is working to ensure that Da'esh cannot gain a new foothold.

Da'esh maintains a presence in various parts of Libya and the ability to conduct asymmetric attacks throughout all of Libya. Da'esh has a presence and has conducted attacks in Benghazi in eastern Libya and Sabratha in western Libya. The Sabratha area has been relatively calm since local militias conducted anti-Da'esh operations there in February and March 2016. Da'esh sleeper cells operate in Tripoli and other cities and towns in Libya.

Ultimately, the best way to eradicate Da'esh in Libya is through building a capable unity government, able to secure Libyan territory and borders. We are working with Libyans and the international community to support the GNA, help Libyans respond to the terrorist threat posed by Da'esh, and de-escalate the conflict in the country. We stand ready to provide humanitarian, economic, and security support to the new Libyan government, upon its request.

Question:

One group in Libya that doesn't receive much outside attention is the "Madkhalis," a Salafi Islamist faction that has been participating in military campaigns against ISIS and has been slowly growing in power. What is the administration's position on the Madkhalis in Libya and what can you tell us about their rise and objectives?

Answer:

The term "Madkhalis" refers to followers of Saudi cleric Rabia bin Hadi al-Madkhali, who promoted a doctrine of obedience to authority. Libyan followers of al-Madkhali's teachings emerged in the early 2000s. Today, there are "Madkhalist" groups in Tripoli, Sirte, and Benghazi.

The U.S. position is that to stabilize the country and keep violent extremists out for the long term, Libya needs to build an inclusive, impartial national security force under the Government of National Accord's (GNA) civilian authority, regardless of ideology. The United States welcomes the Presidency Council's efforts to form a unified, geographically-diverse professional military force and a capable, professional Presidential Guard to protect government institutions and reduce the role of militias in Tripoli.